friends forever

friends forever

what our dogs can teach us about friendship

Words

Mary Ann Long

Pictures

Anna Kuperberg

GOLD ST.
PRESS

best friends
come in all shapes and sizes.

The four-legged kind can teach us a lot about friendship. Dogs are loyal and loving, and they lift our spirits with just a look or a nuzzle. They speak up when something's not right, but they know when to keep quiet, too. They inspire us to get up and go (though sometimes it's just around the block), yet they're also happy chilling out on the couch. They know when to show affection—and they're not stingy with it.

Dogs never take us for granted...and friends don't take each other for granted, either. Through good times and bad, through thick and thin, a true friend is a friend forever.

Just between us...

...I want you to know that you're more to me than just someone to hang out with.

When I need to talk, you're all ears.

Which makes you the perfect confidant—
I know my secrets are safe with you.

You know just how to tickle my funny bone.

When I'm stuck in a corner,
you help me find my way out.

And when things get me down...

...or I'm feeling wiped out...

...you know how to set me straight.

Your wisdom and insight mean a lot to me.

Not only do you have a knack
for getting me back on my feet...

...sometimes you have
me dancing for joy.

So trust me, pal...I've got your back.

Sometimes I pamper you a little,
but a friend like you deserves it.

Whenever we go shopping...

...you find something that's just my style.

You're always up for grabbing a bite...

...and you can make just about anything
special, even hanging around the house.

I miss you when you're not around.

I can't believe some
of the things you've
talked me into doing...

...and vice versa.

Don't worry, I'll never tell!

I treasure the crazy wonderful times we've shared—
and look forward to the adventures to come.

I know we'll always stick together.

You inspire me to be a better person
and love me even when I'm not.

You're my superstar.

You're my hero.

You're my best pal.

I'll be your friend to the very end.

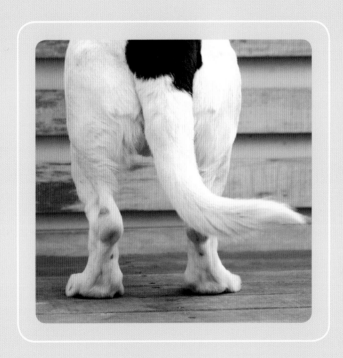

GOLD ST. PRESS

Created and published by Gold Street Press,
an imprint of Weldon Owen Inc. www.goldstreetpress.com

ISBN 13: 978-1-934-533-09-3
ISBN 10: 1-934533-09-2

10 9 8 7 6 5 4 3 2 1

Printed in China